Pebble® Plus

DINOSAURS

STEGOSAURUS

by Tammy Gagne

PEBBLE
a capstone imprint

Pebble Plus is published by Pebble,
1710 Roe Crest Drive, North Mankato, Minnesota 56003
www.mycapstone.com

Library of Congress Cataloging-in-Publication Data
Names: Gagne, Tammy, author.
Title: Stegosaurus : a 4D book / by Tammy Gagne.
Description: North Mankato, Minnesota : an imprint of Pebble, [2019] |
Series: Pebble plus. Dinosaurs | Audience: Age 4–8.
Identifiers: LCCN 2018003052 (print) | LCCN 2018009266 (ebook) |
ISBN 9781515795629 (eBook PDF) | ISBN 9781515795506 (hardcover) |
ISBN 9781515795568 (paperback)
Subjects: LCSH: Stegosaurus—Juvenile literature.
Classification: LCC QE862.O65 (ebook) | LCC QE862.O65 G34 2019 (print)
| DDC 567.915/3—dc23
LC record available at https://lccn.loc.gov/2018003052

Editorial Credits
Hank Musolf, editor; Charmaine Whitman, designer;
Kelly Garvin, media researcher; Laura Manthe, production specialist;
Illustrator, Capstone Press/Jon Hughes

Design Elements
Shutterstock/Krasovski Dmitri

Note to Parents and Teachers

The Dinosaurs set supports the national science standards related to life science. This book describes and illustrates stegosaurus. The images support early readers in understanding the text. The repetition of words and phrases helps early readers learn new words. This book also introduces early readers to subject-specific vocabulary words, which are defined in the Glossary section. Early readers may need assistance to read some words and to use the Table of Contents, Glossary, Read More, Internet Sites, Critical Thinking Questions, and Index sections of the book.

Table of Contents

Meet the Stegosaurus

Stegosaurus was not the biggest or the smallest dinosaur. It was about 30 feet (9 meters) long. This is about the size of a school bus.

Stegosaurus weighed more than 3,500 pounds (1,587 kilograms). It had bony plates down its back. They made this species look bigger.

Stegosaurus had a small head. Its brain was about the size of a hot dog! Scientists do not think the stegosaurus was very smart.

Plant Eaters

Stegosaurus had a beak like a bird. It had round teeth shaped like pegs. But the dinosaur had no front teeth.

This dinosaur was an herbivore. It ate small plants with its weak jaws. Because it had short legs, stegosaurus fed off the ground.

Stegosaurus Bones

Stegosaurus lived about 150 million years ago. This species lived in North America, Europe, Asia, and Africa.

Scientists have found bones of about 80 stegosaurus in the United States. The species likely traveled in herds. These groups had both young and old dinosaurs.

Defending Itself

Stegosaurus could not outrun predators. Short legs made the dinosaur slow. It used its tail to fight off attackers.

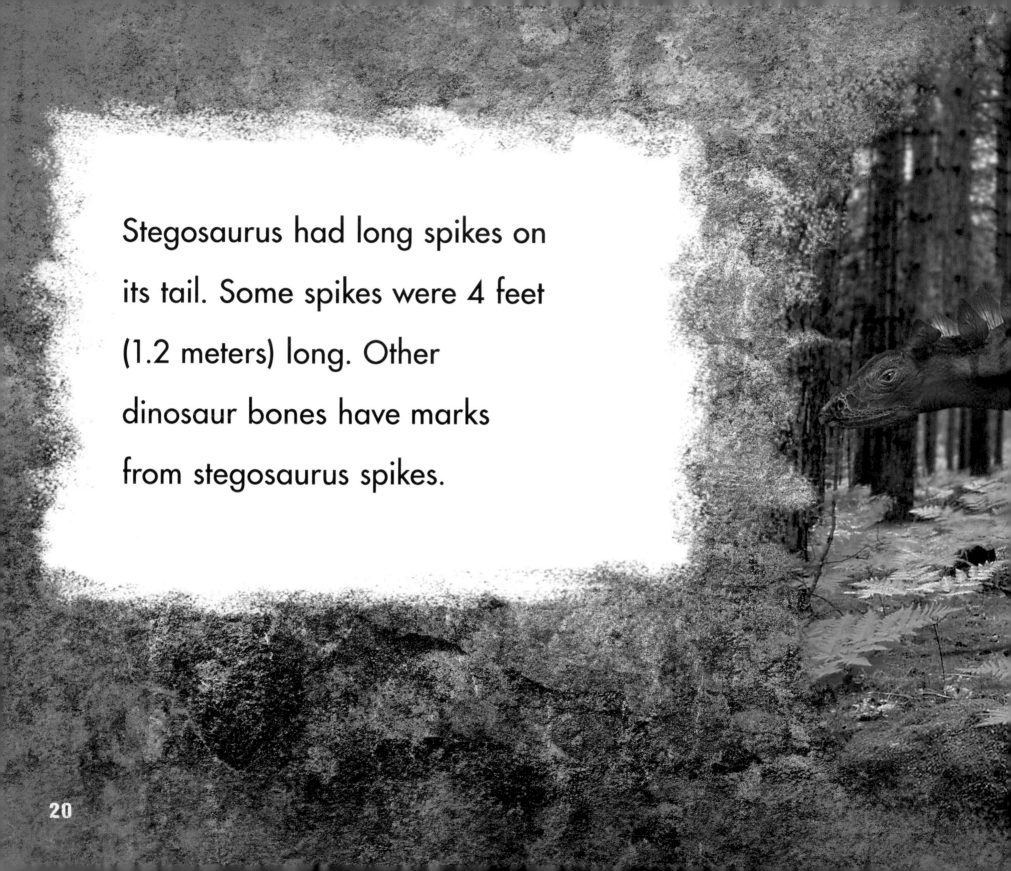

Stegosaurus had long spikes on its tail. Some spikes were 4 feet (1.2 meters) long. Other dinosaur bones have marks from stegosaurus spikes.

Glossary

herbivore—an animal that only eats plants

herd—a group of animals that live and move together

predator—an animal that hunts another animal

scientist—a person who studies the workings of the world

skeleton—the bones of an animal

species—a group of animals who share numerous traits

Read More

Arlon, Penelope and Tory Gordon-Harris. *Dino Safari: A LEGO Adventure in the Real World.* New York: Scholastic, 2016.

Harper, E.T. *Dylan's Amazing Dinosaurs: The Stegosaurus.* Hauppauge, N.Y.: Barron's, 2015.

Wegwerth, A.L. *Stegosaurus.* North Mankato, Minn.: Capstone Press, 2015.

Internet Sites

Use FactHound to find Internet sites related to this book.

Visit www.facthound.com

Just type in 9781515795506 and go.

Check out projects, games and lots more at
www.capstonekids.com

Critical Thinking Questions

1. Do you think other dinosaurs feared the stegosaurus? Why or why not?

2. How do you think scientists know both older and younger Stegosauruses lived in the same herds?

3. Do you think the Stegosaurus could have won fights against predators by biting them? Explain your answer.

Index